PASSPORT *to* HEAVEN

Revised Edition

Marguerite Farison

BARBOUR
PUBLISHING, INC.
Uhrichsville, Ohio

ISBN 1-55748-813-4

Published by Barbour Publishing, Inc.
P.O. Box 719
Uhrichsville, Ohio 44683
http://www.barbourbooks.com

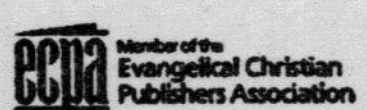

Printed in the United States of America.

Introduction

This is your passport to heaven. Read it carefully and follow the instructions, and you will enjoy safe passage into heaven when the appointed time comes for you to leave this earth.

Information Herein

Your Present Status as a Citizen of Earth

CITIZEN OF EARTH

You became a **TEMPORARY** citizen of **EARTH** when you were born **PHYSICALLY** onto it: "That which is born of the flesh ..." *(John 3:6).*

You were born physically of human parents.

Your **EARTHLY** citizenship ends with your **PHYSICAL DEATH:** "... For the things which are seen are temporal ..." *(2 Corinthians 4:18).*

Your physical body will die.

Your Future Status as a Citizen of Heaven

CITIZEN OF HEAVEN

You become a **PERMANENT** citizen of **HEAVEN** by being born **SPIRITUALLY** into it. ". . . And that which is born of the Spirit is spirit" *(John 3:6).*

This is a spiritual birth, born of God: "Except a man be born again, he cannot see the kingdom of God" *(John 3:3).*

Your citizenship in heaven will never end: "... But the things which are not seen are eternal"

(2 Corinthians 4:18).

The new-born spirit lives forever.

Satan and Hell

BACKGROUND ON SATAN

When God created the universe, He also created millions of angels to be His assistant messengers and helpers. God created one angel, Lucifer, more beautiful, powerful, and intelligent than all the rest, to be their leader *(See: Ezekiel 28:15).*

Lucifer became so proud of himself, he decided he should sit on God's throne and rule the universe. He was able to persuade perhaps as many as one-third of the angels to join him in a colossal double-cross and rebellion against God. *(See: Revelation 12:4)*

In committing this evil act, Lucifer brought himself down to the lowest of all beings. His character and personality changed to pure evil and hate, and he became the ultimate instigator of all sin and evil. He was given a name befitting his new personality, **SATAN,** meaning "enemy, adversary" *(See: Isaiah 14:12-14).*

Satan's other names:

Devil	God of this world
Accuser of the brethren	Prince of devils
Great dragon	Prince of darkness
The evil one	Tempter
Father of lies	Beelzebub
Murderer	Deceiver
Serpent	Prince of the power of the air

The angels who joined him in his rebellion against God became fallen angels, demons, evil spirits, and unclean spirits.

Although Lucifer was very intelligent, he was not all-wise, or he would have realized that the created being (Satan himself) could not overpower and replace his Creator God.

God threw Satan and his demons out of heaven and into hell and onto earth

(See: Luke 10:18; 2 Peter 2:4; Jude 6; Revelation 12:9).

On earth, Satan was allowed to tempt the first man, Adam, who had rulership of the earth. When Adam yielded to Satan's temptation and disobeyed God, he forfeited rulership of the earth over to Satan

(See: Genesis 3:1-24).

Since that time Satan and his demons have had rulership of the earth and its atmosphere *(See: John 12:31; 14:30; 16:11; Ephesians 2:2).*

WHO IS SATAN?

Satan is a created being. He didn't exist until God created him. He is the deceiver and he incites evil in the world. He is God's enemy. He is your enemy.

WHERE IS SATAN?

He operates in hell and the earth and its atmosphere *(See: Job 1:7).*

Satan is not personally present everywhere, as God is.

Satan's demon slaves help give the false impression that he can be everywhere.

WHAT IS SATAN LIKE?

Description of Satan. Satan is very intelligent, but his knowledge is limited. He is not all-wise but is very crafty.

Satan can be invisible.

Satan is powerful, but his power is limited *(See: Ephesians 2:1-6; 6:11, 12).*

Satan is changeable:

Satan changes to suit his purposes.
He is a master of disguise.
He can disguise himself as an angel of light *(See: 2 Corinthians 11:14).*
He can be smooth as silk one minute and like a roaring lion the next.

Satan cannot create — he only corrupts, pollutes, contaminates, and destroys the things God creates. All evil can be traced back to Satan.

Satan is totally false and is a liar and the father of lies.

Satan is arrogant, dishonest, and shameful.

Satan's Personality. According to Job 1:8-11; 2:3-5; Matthew 4:3-11, Satan:

Is rough, wicked and cruel.
Is filled with hate.
Is totally without mercy.
Is utterly selfish.
Has a sick, warped sense of humor.
Is very bitter.
Is jealous of God's power and majesty.
Is rude and arrogant.

Satan's Character. This is what Satan is like. He is:

Totally evil and the instigator of all evil. Not even a fraction of good exists in him.

Proud *(See: Isaiah 14:12-14).*

Unrighteous, totally depraved, and wicked *(See: 1 John 2:13).*

Unholy

Totally corrupt, subtle, and crafty *(See: Genesis 3:1; 2 Corinthians 11:3).*

A liar and the father of lies *(See: 1 Kings 22:21, 22; John 8:44).*

A double-crosser, back stabber, traitor, deceiver *(See: Revelation 20:7, 8; 2 Corinthians 11:14; Ephesians 6:11).*

Totally unjust and unfair.

Cowardly *(See: James 4:7).*

Cruel *(See: Luke 8:29; 9:39, 42).*

A perverter of the Scriptures *(See: Matthew 4:6; Psalms 91:11, 12).*

An opposer of God's work *(See: Zechariah 3:1; 1 Thessalonians 2:18).*

Hindering the Gospel *(See: Matthew 13:19; 2 Corinthians 4:4).*

Satan and his demons hate you with a passion and will use every dirty scheme their evil minds can devise to lure, entice, and trick you down the broad path to the eternal darkness of hell.

Their primary and ultimate goal is to get your eternal soul into hell, where they can torment you throughout eternity.

"Be sober, be vigilant; because your adversary the devil, as a roaring lion, walketh about, seeking whom he may devour"

(1 Peter 5:8).

Satan will try to keep you from making contact with your true Creator, God. If you find God, Satan loses you, and his power over you is broken.

IF YOU CHOOSE SATAN, YOU ARE CHOOSING THE VANQUISHED RULER.

For more information, read: *Satan is Alive and Well on Planet Earth,* by Hal Lindsey.

HELL

Why Is There a Hell? Satan is so evil and powerful that God created hell as an awful place of punishment for Satan and his demons

(See: Matthew 25:41).

Hell is a prison that confines evil beings and prevents them from infecting and contaminating the eternal Kingdom of God with their evil.

Where Is Hell? Hell is a horrible kingdom of torment, possibly located in the bowels of the earth although the Bible does not specifically state the whereabouts of Hades, Hell, or the lake of fire.

Who Rules Over Hell? Satan rules over hell with hatred and cruelty.

What Is Hell Like? First, those in hell will be separated from God, and all God's goodness and love will be totally absent from hell.

Environment:

Everlasting fire *(See: Matthew 13:42; 25:41).*
Darkness *(See: Matthew 22:13; 25:30).*
Chaos.
Later, the lake of fire and brimstone will be a part of hell
(See: Revelation 20:10, 14, 15; 21:8).

TIME: Hell goes on for eternity. Once you are in hell, there is no escape. Those in hell are banished from the living God's presence forever. *(See: Matthew 7:23)*

SPACE: Hell is confinement in a limited space.

GRAVITY: Probably a strong gravitational pull so that movements will be slow.

DWELLINGS: Probably none.

WHO WILL BE IN HELL?

Satan and his demons *(See: Revelation 20:10; Jude 6; 2 Peter 2:4).*

The false prophet and the antichrist (the beast) *(See: Revelation 20:10).*

Those unbelievers who reject God's Son, Jesus, the Messiah *(See: Hebrews 10:26-31, Revelation 21:8).*

The wicked *(Psalm 9:17).*

All things that offend and those who do iniquity *(See: Matthew 13:41, 42).*

The unrighteous: fornicators, idolaters, adulterers, thieves, the covetous, and drunkards, extortioners, murderers, whoremongers, sorcerers, liars, the unjust *(See: Matthew 13:41; Revelation 21:8; 22:11, 15; 1 Corinthians 6:9, 10).*

Whoever's name was not found in the book of life *(See: Revelation 20:15).*

All nations that forget God *(See: Psalm 9:17).*

WHO WILL *NOT* BE IN HELL?

God and His good, faithful angels will not be in hell.

All those who accepted God's Son, Jesus, as their Saviour will not be in hell.

All those whose names are written in the Lamb's book of life will not be in hell.

WHAT WILL THOSE IN HELL BE LIKE?

Body: *Appearance* — Probably contorted because of constant torment.

Health — Conscious suffering forever.

Feelings — Wailing and gnashing of teeth *(See: Matthew 13:42; 22:13; 25:30).*
Tormented day and night for ever and ever *(See: Revelation 20:10).*
There will be eternal pain and suffering but not annihilation.

The body will be resurrected to everlasting contempt and damnation- *(See: Daniel 12:2; John 5:28, 29).*

Clothing: Probably those in hell will be naked.

Mind and Emotions:

MIND

Confusion
Bad thoughts
Error
Boredom and monotony
Mental anguish

EMOTIONS

Mourning, grief, and sorrow
Loneliness
Despair
Anxiety
Hatred, anger, hostility, and animosity
Bitterness and resentment
Envy and jealousy
Frustrations
Regrets and remorse about being in hell instead of heaven.

Immorality

Evil: Hell is chock-full of evil, and eventually it will contain all evil-doers, squeezed into a limited area. Hell will be the eternal habitation of all unrepentant sinners who have committed crime, craftiness, scheming, cheating, and lying ... as well as those who have been guilty of

Backbiting
Hatred, cruelty, and anger
Chaos
Distrust
Discord, conflicts, and fighting
  Dissension
  Laziness
  Cowardice
  Selfishness

Associates: Wicked degenerates will be your associates although there will be no social communication among those in hell.

Government: There will probably be no orderly government but a kind of anarchy. Utter chaos, confusion, injustice and corruption.

Activities in Hell: You can expect:

CRITICISMS and recriminations about your life on earth.
DUTIES: Endurance of perpetual torment and torture.
COMMUNICATION: None.
TRAVEL: Those in hell will not be going anywhere.
EATING: Probably no food or drink.

NOISE: Probably much loud noise — blasphemies, cursing, moaning, groaning, weeping, crying, screaming, and yelling

Those in hell will probably be required to bow and cater to Satan and be his slaves. They may possibly even be required to worship him.

Rewards: There will be no rewards in hell, only punishments.

Everlasting punishment *(See: Matthew 25:46; Isaiah 33:14).*

Shame, contempt, damnation *(See: Daniel 12:2; John 5:29).*

There will be degrees of punishment to match the sins committed *(See: Luke 12:47, 48).*

HOW DO YOU GET INTO HELL?

You were born on this earth a prime candidate for hell.

You do not need a passport to get into hell.

Actually, you can get to hell by doing absolutely nothing: "... for wide is the gate, and broad is the way, that leadeth to destruction, and many there be which go in thereat" *(Matthew 7:13).*

When you were born on this earth, you were born with a sinful nature. This naturally led you into bondage and slavery to Satan. He is your master, and you belong to him unless you have renounced him and committed your life to Jesus Christ *(See: Matthew 13:39-41; 1 John 3:8, 10).*

If you do not choose God's Son, Jesus, then you are automatically choosing Satan and hell. Rejecting Jesus is totally voluntary.

When your body dies, you will plunge into hell with Satan and his demons, and they will gloat over you and harass you.

Once you are in hell, there is no escape.

CONDOLENCES: God has already won the battle with Satan. If you choose hell, you have chosen a defeated kingdom.

You now have an opportunity to invite Jesus into your heart, but if you refuse, then hell is the only place left for you to go after your body dies. No one can enter heaven without Jesus in his heart.

God does not want you in hell. God is not willing that any should perish *(See: 2 Peter 3:9).*

No matter how bad you have been, Jesus can wash you clean.

"Know ye not that the unrighteous shall not inherit the kingdom of God? Be not deceived: neither fornicators, nor idolaters, nor adulterers, nor effeminate, nor abusers of themselves with mankind, Nor thieves, nor covetous, nor drunkards, nor revilers, nor extortioners, shall inherit the kingdom of God. And such were some of you: but ye are washed, but ye are sanctified, but ye are justified in the name of the Lord Jesus, and by the Spirit of our God"

(1 Corinthians 6:9-11).

You can still change your mind and choose God and heaven, but don't wait too long. You can die tomorrow, or even today, and then it's too late.

HEAVEN OR HELL

Because hell is a dark, evil, ugly place of hatred, pain, suffering, torment, sorrow, remorse, chaos, confusion, and eternal confinement, ruled over by slave-master Satan, you must **AVOID** it at all costs

(See: Matthew 25:30, 41, 46).

Because heaven is the place where you want to live forever, and because it has a perfect environment of light, beauty, comfort, happiness, goodness, joy, order, peace, sanity, love, and freedom for eternity, plus you will have a healthy, beautiful body, and all your needs will be provided for you by God, you **MUST ATTAIN** it at all costs.

"But now they desire a better country, that is an heavenly: wherefore God is not ashamed to be called their God: for he hath prepared for them a city" *(Hebrews 11:16).*

HELL IS A DEAD END! Hell is the defeated kingdom.

HEAVEN IS WHERE THE ACTION IS! Heaven is the victorious kingdom.

IN HELL YOU WILL BE PUNISHED FOREVER, ALONG WITH SATAN AND HIS DEMONS.

IN HEAVEN YOU WILL BE REWARDED WITH ALL THE RICHES OF THE UNIVERSE, BY GOD.

A day will come that at the name of Jesus every knee should bow, of things in heaven, and things in earth, and things under the earth; and that every tongue should confess that Jesus Christ is Lord, to the glory of God the Father. *(See: Isaiah 45:23; Romans 14:11; Philippians 2:10, 11).*

CHOOSE LIFE!

How to Become a Citizen of Heaven

NOTICE

YOU MUST BE **BORN** INTO
THE KINGDOM OF HEAVEN.

NO NATURALIZATION
FOR CITIZENSHIP IS PERMITTED.

There is **NO SUCH THING** as a naturalized citizen of heaven.

The naturalization process is **NOT ALLOWED.**

NO visa needed.
NO entry documents needed.
NO residence requirements.
NO age requirements.
NO examination on history and government of heaven required.
NO literacy or education requirements.
NO fingerprints required.
NO witnesses necessary.
NO fee.

NO GOOD WORKS REQUIRED

(See: Ephesians 2:8, 9; Titus 3:5; Isaiah 64:6):

Doing good deeds WON'T get you into heaven.

Trying to be good WON'T get you into heaven.

Going to church WON'T get you into heaven.

Working for the church WON'T get you into heaven.

Giving money to the church, charities, and good causes WON'T get you into heaven.

Merely being water baptized WON'T get you into heaven.

Self-punishment WON'T get you into heaven.

YOU MUST BE BORN INTO THE KINGDOM OF HEAVEN and only God's Son, Jesus, can accomplish this Spiritual Birth.

THIS SPIRITUAL BIRTH MUST TAKE PLACE ON EARTH!

NOTICE

NO ONE MAY ENTER HEAVEN ON ANOTHER PERSON'S CREDENTIALS:

Having Christian parents WON'T get you into heaven.

Having a Christian spouse WON'T get you into heaven.

Having Christian friends WON'T get you into heaven.
Your minister CAN'T get you into heaven.
Your guru CAN'T get you into heaven.
Your church CAN'T get you into heaven.

Anyone who tries to enter heaven through anyone other than Jesus will **FAIL.**

Trying to enter heaven under false sponsorship will result in **FAILURE** and weeping and gnashing of teeth *(See: Luke 13:28).*

"Jesus saith ..., I am the way, the truth, and the life: no man cometh unto the Father, but by me" *(John 14:6).*

"Neither is there salvation in any other; for there is none other name under heaven given among men [Jesus only], whereby we must be saved" *(Acts 4:12).*

Jesus says: "I am the door: by me if any man enter in, he shall be saved, and shall go in and out, and find pasture" *(John 10:9).*

"Because strait is the gate, and narrow is the way, which leadeth unto life, and few there be that find it" *(Matthew 7:14).*

YOU MUST BE BORN INTO THE KINGDOM OF HEAVEN, and only by trusting God's Son, Jesus, can this spiritual birth be accomplished.

THIS SPIRITUAL BIRTH
MUST TAKE PLACE ON EARTH.

HOW TO QUALIFY FOR HEAVENLY CITIZENSHIP

To qualify for heavenly citizenship, you must be **LEGALLY PERFECT** *(See: Matthew 5:20).*

Jesus is the only human being who was **LEGALLY PERFECT.** He was truly MAN and truly GOD. *(See: John 1:14; Romans 1:3, 4; Hebrews 4:14, 15).*

YOU are presently **IMPERFECT** *(See: Romans 3:10, 23).*

YOU DO NOT QUALIFY for heaven.

In order for you to qualify for heavenly citizenship, you must acquire **JESUS' PERFECTION** by becoming **ONE** with **HIM** *(See: John 14:20; Galatians 2:20).*

You can become **ONE** with **JESUS** and acquire **HIS PERFECTION** by inviting **HIM** to come into your heart (spirit) and reside there. He has been waiting all your life for you to invite **HIM** in *(See: Revelation 3:20; John 17:20-23).*

When you invite **HIM** in, **HE** comes in, resides within you, and gives you **HIS PERFECTION.**

This is a spiritual transaction between you and Jesus, known as your spiritual birth. Just as you were **PHYSICALLY** born onto this earth, you must now be **SPIRITUALLY** born into the Kingdom of heaven *(See: John 3:3).*

Your spiritually dead heart, into which you invite Jesus, comes to life when He comes in and resides there. In other words your dead spirit is **BORN OF GOD** *(See: Ephesians 2:1, 5; Colossians 2:13; John 5:26).*

In short, Jesus is your passport to heaven.

TIME LIMIT

You must become a citizen of heaven while you are still living on this earth.

If you die before becoming a citizen of heaven, you will automatically go to hell *(See: John 3:18; Revelation 20:15).*

Since you don't know when you will die, it is vitally important that you become a citizen of heaven immediately.

"... Behold, now is the accepted time; behold, now is the day of salvation" *(2 Corinthians 6:2).*

Don't delay becoming a citizen of heaven. Tomorrow may be too late — later today may be too late. Once you are dead, it's too late to change your eternal destination!

"But God said unto him, Thou fool, this night thy soul shall be required of thee ..."

(Luke 12:20).

"Seek ye the Lord while he may be found, call ye upon him while he is near ..."

(Isaiah 55:6).

PREPARING FOR YOUR SPIRITUAL BIRTH

Please be honest with yourself and with God and admit that you are a sinner.

"If we say that we have no sin, we deceive ourselves, and the truth is not in us"

(1 John 1:8).

"... There is none righteous, no, not one ... For all have sinned and come short of the glory of God" *(Romans 3:10, 23).*

Tell God that you are sorry for your sins.

"God resisteth the proud, but giveth grace unto the humble" *(James 4:6).*

"The Lord is nigh unto them that are of a broken heart; and saveth such as be of a contrite spirit" *(Psalms 34:18).*

"Repent ye therefore, and be converted, that your sins may be blotted out ..."

(Acts 3:19).

Come as a little child in simple faith

(See: Matthew 18:3).

GOD WELCOMES YOU

No one is denied admittance into heaven who truly wants in and is willing to trust Christ.

Jesus says: "... Him that cometh unto me I will in no wise cast out" *(John 6:37)*.

Jesus says: "Behold, I stand at the door, and knock: if any man hear my voice, and open the door, I will come in to him, and will sup with him, and he with me" *(Revelation 3:20)*.

"Ho, every one that thirsteth come ye to the waters ..." *(Isaiah 55:1)*.

"And the Spirit and the bride say, Come, and let him that heareth say, Come. And let him that is athirst come. And whosoever will, let him take the water of life freely" *(Revelation 22:17)*.

"If any man thirst, let him come unto me [Jesus] and drink" *(John 7:37)*.

God says: "And ye shall seek me, and find me, when ye shall search for me with all your heart" *(Jeremiah 29:13)*.

Becoming a Citizen of Heaven

HOW TO BE BORN INTO THE KINGDOM OF HEAVEN

YOU SAY — preferably aloud: "Jesus, I believe that You are the Christ and God raised You from the dead" *(Romans 10:9, 10).*

"Jesus come into my heart and become one with me and give me Your **NEW LIFE.**"

When you sincerely invite Jesus into your heart, He comes in. When Jesus comes into your heart, you are born into the kingdom of heaven.

The moment you receive Jesus into your heart, Jesus receives you into His kingdom of heaven *(See: John 1:12; Matthew 7:7, 8; 28:18).*

YOU SAY — preferably aloud: "Jesus, I accept you as my King as I come into Your kingdom of heaven."

You are now a born-again citizen of heaven.

YOU SAY: "Thank You, Jesus, for coming into my heart and giving me Your perfection and receiving me into Your kingdom" *(See: 2 Corinthians 5:21).*

CONGRATULATIONS, you have just completed the most important transaction of your life. It determines where (heaven) and with whom (God) you will spend eternity (forever).

YOU HAVE CHOSEN ETERNAL LIFE IN THE VICTORIOUS KINGDOM.

YOU ARE NOW A CITIZEN OF HEAVEN

On the authority of the Bible, and with the privilege vested in me as a Christian believer: I now pronounce you to be a citizen of heaven, with full and immediate rights and privileges of citizenship while you are still on earth, and when your body dies you will be escorted into heaven by God and His angels

(See: Ephesians 2:19; Philippians 3:20).

God and the angels in heaven are rejoicing as you become a citizen of heaven

(See: Luke 15:7).

All your loved ones in heaven are also rejoicing.

You may now fill out your spiritual birth certificate and your passport to heaven.

Please understand, this paper passport is not necessary for you to enter heaven but is a record for you, to make the transaction more real to you and to give you reassurance when doubts come to you about your new-birth experience.

CERTIFICATE OF SPIRITUAL BIRTH

This certifies that ______________________ 's
Name

dead spirit was brought to newness of life by Jesus at ____________________ o'clock on the
Time

__________ of __________, ______ A.D.
Day Month Year

(this is your spiritual birthday.)

in ________________, ________________,
City State

at ____________ years of age.
Age

Father is: God the Father
Sponsor is: God the Son
Witness is: God the Holy Spirit

Other witnesses, if any ________________.
Optional

This birth certificate verifies that you have been born into the kingdom of heaven and are now a CITIZEN OF HEAVEN, having met the requirement of RIGHTEOUSNESS when your new birth made you ONE with Jesus.

Properly Fill in Blanks

PASSPORT TO HEAVEN

THIS PASSPORT CERTIFIES THAT

____

Your Name

has been born into the kingdom of heaven and has met the requirement of RIGHTEOUSNESS for full citizenship by becoming **ONE** with Jesus, and is now a first-class citizen of heaven, with all the rights and privileges thereof.

Your name is now written in the Lamb's book of life.

____

Date this Passport Becomes Valid
(The Same Date as Your Spiritual Birth)

____

Your Address

YOUR

PICTURE

(Optional)

____

Date Water Baptized
(Fill in Later)

Expiration date: **NONE.**

IMPORTANT PASSPORT INFORMATION

Expiration. This is a lifetime passport and is valid forever — NO expiration date.

Surrender. This passport is your own private property and need never be surrendered.

Loss, Theft, or Destruction of This Passport. A new passport can be purchased at Christian bookstores, or you can write up a new one yourself.

Alteration or Mutilation of This Passport. Once this passport has been properly filled out, it need not be changed. Since it is the record of your citizenship in heaven you undoubtedly will take proper care of it.

Amendments, Endorsements, and Modifications. NO amendments or endorsements will be necessary.

Visas. NO visas will be required in the kingdom of heaven. Your passport assures you that you have met all the requirements and are a bona fide citizen of heaven.

Restrictions. NO one may enter heaven on another person's credentials. Each person must enter on his own oneness with Christ Jesus.

Notice. Possession of this physical passport is not necessary for entry into heaven, but possession of the Holy Spirit and Jesus and God the Father is necessary for heavenly entrance. This passport is merely your reassurance that you are a citizen of heaven after you have been born anew.

YOUR PRESENT STATUS AS A CITIZEN OF HEAVEN AND A CITIZEN OF EARTH

With Jesus dwelling in your newborn spirit, you are now a full-fledged citizen of heaven, with many immediate privileges and benefits here on earth and many more future privileges and benefits in heaven.

You are still a citizen of earth by virtue (reason) of your physical birth onto earth and your present residence here.

At the same time you are also a citizen of heaven by reason (virtue) of your spiritual birth into heaven *(See: Luke 17:21).*

You are now a DUAL citizen of both heaven and earth, with all the privileges and responsibilities of both.

You are now a **DUAL NATIONAL,** with citizenship in two countries. The physical realm of earth, ruled by Satan, and the spiritual and physical realm of heaven, ruled by God.

You owe allegiance to two countries at the same time and are subject to the laws of both countries.

The rulership of your life has now changed from Satan to God *(Acts 26:18).* God is now your Father, King, and Lord, and your first and primary allegiance is to Him

(See: Matthew 6:24; Ephesians 2:1-10).

Obey the Laws of Earth (See: 1 Peter 2:13, 14, 17). "And Jesus answering said unto them, Render to Caesar the things that are Caesar's, and to God the things that are God's ..."

(Mark 12:17).

Obey the Laws of Heaven. See pages 71 - 75: "... A Good Citizen of Heaven: Obeys and Serves God."

LOSS OF NATIONALITY

You will not lose your heavenly nationality by being a citizen of earth or by taking an oath or making a declaration of allegiance to, or by serving in the armed forces or accepting employment under the government of earth

(See: John 10:28, 29).

For detailed information, consult your Heavenly Citizenship Manual (the Bible)

(See: 1 Peter 2:13, 14, 17).

Prolonged Residence Abroad. No matter how long you reside on earth, you will not lose your heavenly citizenship, and you do not need to register your whereabouts. God knows where you are.

Your heavenly citizenship can never be taken from you.

If difficulties occur, consult your Heavenly Citizenship Manual.

COMMITMENT

I declare that I will support and defend the laws of heaven against all enemies, foreign and domestic, that I will bear true faith and allegiance to the same and that I take this obligation freely, without any mental reservation or purpose of evasion; so help me God.

HEAVENLY CITIZENSHIP CREED (THE APOSTLES' CREED)

I believe in God the Father Almighty, maker of heaven and earth; and in Jesus Christ, his only Son, our Lord, who was conceived by the Holy Ghost, born of the Virgin Mary, suffered under Pontius Pilate, was crucified, dead, and buried. He descended into Hell; the third day he rose again from the dead; he ascended into heaven, and sitteth on the right hand of God, the Father Almighty, From thence he shall come to judge the living and the dead.

I believe in the Holy Ghost, the Church as the Body of Christ, consisting of all Believers in Union with Christ, the Oneness of Believers in Christ, the forgiveness of sins, the resurrection of the body, and the life everlasting.

Amen.

Status, Privileges, and Benefits of Heavenly Citizenship While Still on Earth

NEW STATUS OF YOUR SPIRIT AND ETERNAL LIFE

Your DEAD SPIRIT has been BROUGHT TO LIFE *(See: Ephesians 2:1, 5; Colossians 2:13; John 5:24).*

You now have a BODY, SOUL, and LIVING SPIRIT.

You now possess ETERNAL LIFE, because Jesus has conquered death for you *(See: John 3:16; 11:25, 26; 14:19; 1 John 5:11-13).*

YOUR SPIRIT WILL NEVER DIE: That is, your personality, mind, emotions, will, and newborn spirit will live forever.

JESUS, the SON, and GOD, the FATHER, are residing in your newborn spirit (heart) *(See: John 14:20; 17:20-23; 1 John 4:15).*

YOUR NEW RELATIONSHIP TO GOD, HIS FAMILY, AND HIS ANGELS

God is your Father *(See: John 1:12, 13).*

Jesus is your Brother and Friend *(See: John 15:13-15).*

God the Holy Spirit is with you *(See: John 14:17).*

You are now a child of God *(See: John 1:12).*

You are now a member of the family of God *(See: Ephesians 3:15).*

You are now a member of Christ's Body, the Church *(See: 1 Corinthians 12:12-14, 27).*

All Christian believers both on earth and in heaven are your brothers and sisters in Christ *(See: Matthew 12:50; Galatians 3:26).*

The angels are your guardians and protectors *(See: Psalm 34:7).*

You are now a citizen of heaven *(See: Ephesians 2:19).*

YOUR NEW LEGAL STATUS IN CHRIST

You are now legally united with Jesus *(See: 2 Corinthians 5:21).*

You are now legally righteous, pure, and blameless. All your sins, past, present, and future are forgiven and washed away by Jesus' blood *(See: 1 John 1:7; 1 Peter 1:18, 19, 23; 1 Corinthians 6:11; Isaiah 1:18; 53:6; Colossians 2:9-17).*

You are a saint *(See: Romans 1:7; Colossians 1:2; 1 Corinthians 1:2; 2 Corinthians 1:1).*

You are a priest *(See: 1 Peter 2:9; Revelation 1:6; 5:10; 20:6).*

You are a totally new person, born from above *(See: 1 John 5:1; Colossians 3:9, 10; 1 Corinthians 5:7).*

NEW PRIVILEGES IN CHRIST

You now belong to Jesus and are under His protection *(See: John 10:28, 29; Ephesians 6:13-18).*

Jesus will never leave you or forsake you *(See: Hebrews 13:5).*

Jesus will confess your name before God the Father and before His angels *(See: Matthew 10:32; Luke 12:8).*

You have direct access to God the Father through Jesus *(See: Romans 5:1, 2).*

You may make requests to God the Father in Jesus' name *(See: John 14:13, 14; 15:16; 16:23, 24, 26).*

Your name is written in the Lamb's book of life *(See: Revelation 3:5; 20:15; Luke 10:20).*

God has a perfect plan for your life *(See: Romans 9:11).*

You must let God guide you in it, to make all things work together for good *(See: Romans 8:28).*

You may ask for and receive the Infilling of the Holy Spirit *(See: Matthew 3:11; Luke 11:13).*

You May Trust All God's Promises. The Bible is full of promises to citizens of heaven, and you can have a treasure hunt going through the Bible and discovering all God's promises *(2 Peter 1:4)*.

Here are a few promises to get you started (notice many of them have conditions attached; I have emphasized the conditions):

"*Come unto me,* all ye that labour and are heavy laden, and I will give you rest" *(Matthew 11:28)*.

"And whatsoever ye shall *ask in my name* [Jesus], that will I do, that the Father may be glorified in the Son. If ye shall *ask* any thing *in my name,* I [Jesus] will do it" *(John 14:13, 14)*.

"If any of you lack wisdom, *let him ask of God,* that giveth to all men liberally, and upbraideth not; and it shall be given him, But *let him ask in faith, nothing wavering*. For he that wavereth is like a wave of the sea driven with the wind and tossed" *(James 1:5, 6)*.

"*Delight thyself also in the Lord;* and he shall give thee the desires of thine heart" *(Psalm 37:4)*.

"Thou wilt keep him in perfect peace, *whose mind is stayed on thee: because he trusteth in thee*" *(Isaiah 26:3)*.

"Casting all your care upon him; for he careth for you" *(1 Peter 5:7).*

NEW STATUS CONCERNING THE LAW

You are no longer under the law of Moses but are now under the law of grace and faith and the Spirit.

Jesus puts the law in your heart when He indwells you with the Holy Spirit *(See: Ezekiel 36:26; Hebrews 8:10).*

Jesus came not to destroy the law but to fulfill the law *(See: Matthew 5:17, 18).*

Jesus fulfilled the law by obeying it perfectly and paying the full penalty of the law by His death. Jesus' shed blood covers your inability and failure to keep the complete law perfectly. Jesus took the judgment of your sin upon Himself *(See: Romans 8:1; 1 Peter 1:18, 19).*

A CHANGED RELATIONSHIP WITH SATAN

You are now free from bondage and slavery to Satan *(See: Acts 26:18; Luke 4:18; John 8:36; Ephesians 4:8).*

Jesus has released you from Satan's dominion, sin, and death *(See: Matthew 20:28; Acts 26:18; 2 Timothy 2:26; John 8:36; Hebrews 2:14, 15).*

Jesus protects you from attacks by Satan and his demons. When you call on Jesus for help, He helps you resist temptations. You may now rebuke and defeat Satan in the Name of Jesus *(See: Mark 16:17).*

Jesus is your representative before the Father when Satan accuses you *(See: Revelation 12:10; Romans 8:34; Hebrews 7:25; 1 John 2:1).*

Your SIN NATURE IS LEGALLY DEFEATED but is still alive and powerful *(See: Romans 6:6; Colossians 3:9, 10; Ephesians 4:22).*

You now have TWO NATURES within you that are at war with each other:

1. The OLD SIN NATURE, which draws you to your earthly kingdom and to your worldly desires and temptations.

2. Your NEW CHRIST-LIKE NATURE, which draws you to your heavenly kingdom and to your eternal destiny.

These TWO NATURES will continue to struggle within you, but if you follow the "Duties and Responsibilities of Good Heavenly Citizenship" (pages 61 - 88), your new godly nature will be in control most of the time. When your body dies, your old sin nature will die with it, and only your Christ-like nature will go with you into heaven

(See: Romans 7:22-25).

Satan,
Your Former Ruler,
Is Now Your Enemy

RENOUNCING SATAN

You must now RENOUNCE Satan, your former ruler, and any and all direct association you have ever had with him and his demons *(See: Isaiah 14:12-17; Ezekiel 28:12-15).*

YOU SAY: "I hereby declare that I absolutely and entirely renounce and disavow all allegiance and fidelity to the prince of darkness, Satan, and his demons with whom I have heretofore been associated."

Mention any specific associations that come to mind.

THE FOLLOWING ARE EXAMPLES OF SATANIC AND DEMONIC ACTS AND ACTIVITIES:

Cults. All religions and/or churches that **DENY** that Jesus is the Son of God who died for our sins and was raised bodily from the grave, walked the earth forty days, then ascended into heaven, and now sits on the right hand of God the Father and IS God the Son *(See: Acts 1:1-3; 1 Corinthians 15:4-8; Acts 4:10-12; Ephesians 1:20-23).*

"But though we, or an angel from heaven, preach any other gospel unto you than that which we have preached unto you, let him be accursed" *(See: Galatians 1:8; 2 Corinthians 11:14).*

"For many deceivers are entered into the world, who confess not that Jesus Christ is come in the flesh. This is a deceiver and an antichrist" *(2 John 7).*

"If there come any unto you, and bring not this doctrine, receive him not into your house, neither bid him God speed: For he that biddeth him God speed is partaker of his evil deeds" *(2 John 10, 11; See: 2 Corinthians 11:13-15).*

"Beloved, believe not every spirit, but try the spirits whether they are of God: because many false prophets are gone out into the world. Hereby know ye the Spirit of God: Every spirit that confesseth that Jesus Christ is come in the flesh is of God: And every spirit that confesseth not that Jesus Christ is come in the flesh is not of God: and this is that spirit of antichrist, whereof ye have heard that it should come; and even now already is it in the world" *(1 John 4:1-3).*

Occult. These also are Satanic and demonic:

Astral projection
Levitation
Telekinesis
Divination
(See: Acts 16:16-18)
Fortune-telling

Extrasensory perception
Telepathy
Mind reading
Clairvoyance
Psychics
Parapsychology
Metaphysics
Numerology
Water witching
Spiritism *(See: Deuteronomy 18:10-12)*
Mediums and seances
Hypnotism
Transcendental meditation
Drugs *(See: Chronicles 10:13; Isaiah 8:19; Leviticus 19:31; 20:6)*
Demon worship
Visions
Crystal balls
Pendulums
Card reading
Palm reading
Tea-leaf reading
Ouija boards
Astrology
Handwriting analysis
Black magic
Sorcery *(See: Acts 13:6-12)*
Witchcraft *(See: Revelation 21:8)*
Serpent charming
Hexing
Angel worship *(See: Colossians 2:18)*
Satan worship *(See: Revelation 9:20)*

Please destroy all articles, books, and paraphernalia that you possess pertaining to any of the above *(See: Acts 19:13-20)*.

Addictions. These destructive habits are often encouraged by Satan:

Nicotine
Alcohol
Continued evil and negative thoughts

STEPS

4

I AM BAD
MY SIN
THE WAGES OF SI
DEATH - ROMANS
ALL HAVE SINNED -
ROMANS 3 : 23

HRIST DIED FOR
S- ROMANS 5:8

DID YOU CLIMB THE STEPS ?

PRAY.....

"JESUS, I AM BAD.
MY SIN KEEPS ME
FROM YOU – BUT YOU
DIED FOR ME.
I AM SORRY I HAVE
SINNED. JESUS, COME
INTO MY HEART AND
BE MY LORD AND SAVIOUR. AMEN."

I'M SAVED

....

WRITE YOUR NAME ON THE LINE.
GOD WILL WRITE YOUR NAME IN
THE 'BOOK OF LIFE' IN HEAVEN.

FREE TRACT SOCIETY
6012 York Blvd. • P.O. Box 42544
Los Angeles, CA 90042 • Los Angeles, CA 90050
This ministry maintained by the gifts of God's people

Drugs
Food overindulgence
Gambling
Bad temper
Continued evil and negative deeds

Addictions are any habits that allow you to lose control of yourself. Satan encourages addictions because these make you vulnerable to obsession, control, and possession by Satan and his demons.

All of the above on this page and the previous page make you vulnerable to influence, obsession and possession by Satan and evil spirits (demons) *(See: Luke 4:41; 8:2, 26-29, 22:3; Acts 5:3; Ephesians 2:2; Matthew 4:24; 8:16, 28, 33; John 13:27; Mark 1:32-34; 5:12).*

For further information on this subject, I recommend the book *Satan Is Alive and Well on Planet Earth* by Hal Lindsey.

PROTECTION FROM SATAN

PUT ON YOUR SPIRITUAL ARMOUR.

"Put on the whole armour of God, that ye may be able to stand against the wiles of the devil. For we wrestle not against flesh and blood, but against principalities, against powers, against the rulers of the darkness of this world, against spiritual wickedness in high places. Wherefore take unto you the whole armour of God, that ye may be able to withstand in the evil day, and having done all, to stand. Stand therefore, having your loins girt about with truth, and having on the breastplate of righteousness; And your feet shod with the preparation of the gospel of peace; Above all, taking the shield of faith, wherewith ye shall be able to quench all the fiery darts of the wicked. And take the helmet of salvation, and the sword of the spirit, which is the word of God" *(Ephesians 6:11-17).*

RESIST SATAN.

"Be sober, be vigilant; because your adversary the devil, as a roaring lion, walketh about, seeking whom he may devour. Whom resist stedfast in the faith, knowing that the same afflictions are accomplished in your brethren that are in the world" *(1 Peter 5:8, 9; See: James 4:7).*

REBUKE SATAN IN JESUS' NAME.

Jesus rebuked Satan: "Get thee behind me, Satan; thou art an offence unto me" *(Matthew 16:23; Mark 8:33; Luke 4:8).*

DEFEAT SATAN.

You defeat Satan when you praise God. *(Read aloud Psalm 148 or sing the doxology "Gloria Patri").*

You defeat Satan when you quote Scripture.

> The Word of God is the sword of the spirit *(See: Ephesians 6:17).*
>
> Jesus said: "It is written" *(See: Matthew 4:1-11; Luke 4:1-13).*

In Jesus' name, take authority over Satan and his demons, and command them to leave *(See: Mark 16:17; Acts 16:18).*

TRAVEL IN DISTURBED AREAS

Travel is restricted in the following areas where Satan and his demons have a stronghold and are especially active and where God is NOT welcome!

Where false religion is being practiced.

Where witchcraft and occult activities are practiced.

Places where God is denounced and where worship of God is forbidden or discouraged.

Adult bookstores, X-rated movies, bars, adult video shops, houses of prostitution, and massage parlors.

Places where crime and dishonesty are encouraged and accepted as normal.

If you inadvertently find yourself in these places:

GET OUT, FAST, unless you are witnessing for Jesus Christ in these areas.

In case of backsliding and sin, notify:

God the Father
God the Son
God the Holy Spirit

Also notify:

____

Your Church Name and Address

____

Your Pastor and/or Spiritual Counselor

Missionaries are an exception. As they go into heathen countries, they can count on God's protection from Satan and his demons. Christians should be spiritually strong and clothed in the whole armor of God, before entering this area of service.

Being Filled With the Holy Spirit

THE FULLNESS OF THE HOLY SPIRIT

Jesus has SOMETHING MORE for you!

Jesus wants to fill you on a daily basis with His Presence, God the Holy Spirit
(See: John 14:16, 17, 26; Matthew 3:11; Acts 2:38).

The Holy Spirit dwelt in Jesus while He was on earth. Now that Jesus has ascended into heaven, He sends the Holy Spirit to those who ask for Him.

YOU SAY — preferably aloud:

"Jesus, please fill me with God the Holy Spirit. I willingly place myself under Your full control" *(See: Luke 11:9-13).*

Jesus does *(See: Matthew 3:11; John 1:32, 33).*

YOU SAY — preferably aloud:

"Thank You, Jesus, for filling me with God the Holy Spirit."

As you accept Jesus as Master of your life, He fills you with His Presence. God the Holy Spirit now controls your newborn spirit. You will remain filled as long as you continue to obey His will and His Word.

God the Holy Spirit now gives you the FRUIT ... and GIFTS of the Spirit.

"But ye shall receive power, after that the Holy Ghost is come upon you ..." *(Acts 1:8).*

THE FRUIT AND GIFTS OF THE HOLY SPIRIT

YOU NOW POSSESS THE **FRUIT** OF THE SPIRIT *(See: Galatians 5:22, 23).*

The FRUIT of the Spirit grow in you in proportion to your obedience and submission to the Holy Spirit and your study of your Citizenship Manual (Bible) and your continuous communication (prayer) with your King (God) *(See: John 15:5, 7).*

Walk in the Spirit *(See: Galatians 5:16-25; Romans 8:14).*

FRUIT OF GOD THE HOLY SPIRIT
(See: Galatians 5:22, 23).

Love (agape; unconditional)	Kindness
	Faithfulness
Joy	Goodness
Peace	Humility
Patience	Discipline (self-control)

God's Law becomes written in your heart (spirit) *(See: Jeremiah 31:33; Hebrews 8:10).*

YOU NOW POSSESS CERTAIN **GIFTS** OF THE SPIRIT *(See: 1 Corinthians 12:7-11).*

God the Holy Spirit activates the gifts of the Spirit in you as He chooses and as needed.

GIFTS OF GOD THE HOLY SPIRIT

(See: 1 Corinthians 12:7-11).

The word of wisdom
The word of knowledge
Gift of faith
Gifts of healing
The working of miracles
Gift of prophecy
The discerning of spirits
Gift of tongues
The interpretation of tongues
Other ministry gifts
(See: Romans 12: 6-8 and Ephesians 4:8)

THE *WORK* OF THE HOLY SPIRIT

The Holy Spirit's WORK is to glorify Jesus and to transform you into Christ's image so that your ACTUAL status is equal to your LEGAL status.

The Father and the Son WORK by and through the Holy Spirit.

The Holy Spirit inspired the Scriptures *(See: 2 Timothy 3:16; 2 Peter 1:21).*

He was active in creation *(See: Genesis 1:2).*

He glorifies Jesus *(See: John 16:14).*

He brings Jesus' Words to your remembrance *(See: John 14:26).*

He convicts you of sin *(See: John 16:8-11).*

He guides you *(See: John 16:13).*

He intercedes for you in prayer *(See: Romans 8:26).*
He testifies of Christ *(See: John 15:26).*
He leads you *(See: Acts 8:29; Romans 8:14).*
He commands *(See: Acts 16:6, 7).*
He comforts you *(See: John 14:26; Acts 9:31).*
He teaches you *(See: John 14:26; 1 Corinthians 12:3).*

In summary, the Holy Spirit is your Helper, and He equips you for service.

YOU ARE NOW THE TEMPLE OF GOD

(See: 1 Corinthians 3:16, 17)

All three PERSONS of the Godhead are dwelling inside your newborn spirit.

God the Father *(See: John 14:23)*
God the Son *(See: John 14:20, 23)*
God the Holy Spirit *(See: John 14:16, 17)*

With the three Persons of the Godhead dwelling inside you, you are ready to embark on your Christian walk as a new citizen of the kingdom of heaven *(See: 1 John 3:24; 4:12-16).*

Recommended books on the Holy Spirit:

The Holy Spirit and You, by Dennis and Rita Bennett

The Helper, by Catherine Marshall.

The Holy Spirit, by Billy Graham.

Duties and Responsibilities of Heavenly Citizenship While Residing on Earth

EXPLANATION

As a citizen of EARTH you have certain duties and responsibilities.

As a citizen of HEAVEN you also have certain duties and responsibilities.

As a DUAL citizen of both earth and heaven you have responsibilities to both heaven and earth.

Keep in mind that your duties and responsibilities as a citizen of heaven are a privilege and a blessing.

On the following pages are some guides to becoming a good citizen of heaven while still on earth.

This is your CITIZENSHIP TRAINING.

This training helps you become spiritually mature so that you can carry your share of responsibilities on earth and also in the heavenly kingdom.

A GOOD CITIZEN OF HEAVEN IS: WATER BAPTIZED

WATER BAPTISM is the physical confirmation of your spiritual birth. It is the acting out of the spiritual transaction.

As your body is lowered into the water you are identifying with Jesus' death and burial as well as symbolizing the death of your old worldly self. As your body is lifted out of the water you are identifying with Jesus' resurrection and symbolizing your new spiritual birth and your oneness with Jesus

(See: Colossians 2:12, 13; Romans 6:3, 4).

It also symbolizes your future resurrection from the dead, as well as symbolizing your inner cleansing.

Repent and be baptized *(See: Acts 2:38; Matthew 3:6).*

Believe that Jesus Christ is the Son of God and be baptized

(See: Acts 8:36-39; 18:8).

Jesus is baptized *(See: Matthew 3:13-17; Luke 3:21, 22).*

Baptize in the name of the Father, and the Son, and of the Holy Ghost *(See: Matthew 28:19; Acts 10:48).*

A GOOD CITIZEN OF HEAVEN: TAKES COMMUNION

Eating the BREAD symbolizes partaking of Christ's BODY, broken for you.

"And he took bread, and gave thanks, and brake it, and gave unto them, saying, This is my body which is given for you: this do in remembrance of me" *(Luke 22:19; See: Matthew 26:26; Mark 14:22; 1 Corinthians 11:23, 24).*

Drinking the WINE symbolizes partaking of Christ's BLOOD, shed for you.

"Likewise also the cup after supper, saying, This cup is the new testament in my blood, which is shed for you" *(Luke 22:20; See: Matthew 26:27-29; Mark 14:23-25; 1 Corinthians 11:25-34).*

Guidance for the Lord's Table (Communion) *(See: 1 Corinthians 11).*

A GOOD CITIZEN OF HEAVEN: COMMUNICATES WITH GOD

You were dead in your sin and could not communicate with God, but you NOW have a LIVE SPIRIT in which God the Father, God the Son, and God the Holy Spirit dwell, and you can communicate with God at all times and in all places. You now have the marvelous privilege of conversing with God.

God SPEAKS to you through HIS WORD, the BIBLE, and through your SPIRIT and MIND.

You SPEAK to God through PRAYER.

Reading the Bible and praying are CONVERSING with God.

Now that you can hear God and speak to God, take full advantage of this marvelous privilege.

A GOOD CITIZEN OF HEAVEN: LISTENS TO GOD

God SPEAKS to you through His Word, the BIBLE.

The Bible is your Citizenship Manual, written by God the Holy Spirit. When you read the Bible, you are listening to God. God tells you what He expects of you and what you can expect from Him.

You should read, believe, study, meditate, memorize, and obey God's Word daily.

THE BIBLE, GOD'S WORD:

> "Sanctify them through thy truth: thy word is truth" *(John 17:17).*
>
> "For the prophecy came not in old time by the will of man: but holy men of God spake as they were moved by the Holy Ghost" *(2 Peter 1:21).*

"All scripture is given by inspiration of God, and is profitable for doctrine, for reproof, for correction, for instruction in righteousness" *(2 Timothy 3:16, 17).*

"And he [Jesus] answered and said, "It is written, man shall not live by bread alone, but by every word that proceedeth out of the mouth of God" *(Matthew 4:4; Luke 4:4; Deuteronomy 8:3).*

"The grass withereth, the flower fadeth: but the word of our God shall stand forever" *(Isaiah 40:8).*

"Thy words were found, and I did eat them; and thy word was unto me the joy and rejoicing of mine heart ..." *(Jeremiah 15:16).*

"How sweet are thy words unto my taste! ... yea, sweeter than honey to my mouth!" *(Psalms 119:103).*

"Thy word is a lamp unto my feet, and a light unto my path" *(Psalms 119:105)*

"For the word of God is quick, and powerful, and sharper than any twoedged sword, piercing even to the dividing asunder of soul and spirit, and of the joints and marrow, and is a discerner of the thoughts and intents of the heart" *(Hebrews 4:12).*

God SPEAKS to you through your Spirit and Mind.

As well as SPEAKING to you through His Word, God also SPEAKS to you through your spirit and mind, so listen for His voice; be sure it is God SPEAKING and not Satan.

If what you hear conflicts with what God tells you in His Word, then you know it is not from God. God never contradicts Himself.

When Man LISTENS, God SPEAKS. "Speak, Lord; for thy servant heareth ..."

(1 Samuel 3:9, 10).

God SPEAKS to you through Jesus' WORDS and LIFE.

Jesus is the LIVING WORD. "In the beginning was the Word and the Word was with God, and the Word was God" *(John 1:1; Revelation 19:13).* "And the Word was made flesh and dwelt among us ..." *(John 1:14).*

Study a number of Bible translations, versions, and paraphrases.

Some good ones are:

Scofield Reference Bible; King James Version; Revised Standard Version; The Living Bible; New International Version; New American Standard Bible; and the New King James Version.

Suggested Bible Reference Books and Helps:

What the Bible is All About, by Henrietta Mears

Halley's Bible Handbook.

Cruden's Complete Concordance.

The New Compact Bible Dictionary.

Wycliffe Bible Commentary.

A GOOD CITIZEN OF HEAVEN: TALKS TO GOD

TALKING to God is called PRAYING.

You can TALK to God silently in your mind (He knows your thoughts), and you can also TALK to Him aloud. You will probably use both methods.

TALK everything over with God. He loves you and wants to be involved in every moment and every activity of your life.

Remember God made you and has been watching over you closely since the moment you were conceived. He knows everything you've ever thought, said, and done and loves you anyway. He knows what is best for you, so always ask Him for advice on every aspect of your life. He actually knows more about you than you yourself do.

Be totally honest and open with God. Remember, He loves you and you can trust Him. Don't ever lie to God or try to con Him.

Christ's pattern for prayer: *See: Matthew 6:9-13; Luke 11:1-4.* For more information on prayer read *A Layman Looks at the Lord's Prayer,* by W. Phillip Keller.

Read the prayers of David in the Psalms. David knew how to pray.

PRAY WITHOUT CEASING

(See: 1 Thessalonians 5:17).

"Give ear to my prayer, O God; and hide not thyself from my supplication"

(Psalm 55:1).

"Evening, and morning, and at noon, will I pray, and cry aloud: and he shall hear my voice" *(Psalm 55:17).*

"Hearken unto the voice of my cry, my King, and my God: for unto thee will I pray"

(Psalm 5:3)

PRAY FOR WISDOM AND GUIDANCE

(See: James 1:5; Proverbs 3:5, 6).

The HOLY SPIRIT, who lives inside you will help you pray *(See: Ephesians 6:18).*

"Likewise the Spirit also helpeth our infirmities: for we know not what we should pray for as we ought: but the Spirit itself maketh intercession for us with groanings which cannot be uttered. And he that searcheth the hearts knoweth what is the mind of the Spirit, because he maketh intercession for the saints according to the will of God" *(Romans 8:26, 27).*

PRAYERS OF PRAISE AND ADORATION

"By him therefore let us offer the sacrifice of praise to God continually, that is, the fruit of our lips giving thanks to his name" *(Hebrews 13:15).*

"Seven times a day do I praise thee because of thy righteous judgments" *(Psalm 119:164).*

"Let every thing that hath breath praise the Lord. Praise ye the Lord" *(Psalm 150:6).*

For more about praise, read all the *Praise* books by Merlin Carothers.

PRAYERS OF THANKS

"Giving thanks always for all things unto God and the Father in the name of our Lord Jesus Christ" *(Ephesians 5:20).*

"In every thing give thanks: for this is the will of God in Christ Jesus concerning you" *(1 Thessalonians 5:18).*

PRAYERS OF INTERCESSION

"Is any sick among you? Let him call for the elders of the church; and let them pray over him, anointing him with oil in the name of the Lord: And the prayer of faith shall save the sick, and the Lord shall raise him up; and if he have committed sins, they shall be forgiven him. Confess your faults one to another, and pray one for another, that ye may be healed. The effectual fervent prayer of a righteous man availeth much" *(James 5:14-16).*

"I exhort therefore, that first of all, supplications, prayers, intercessions, and giving of thanks, be made for all men; For kings, and for all that are in authority; that we may lead a quiet and peaceable life in all godliness and honesty" *(1 Timothy 2:1, 2).*

PRAYERS OF REQUEST

"Therefore I say unto you, What things soever ye desire, when ye pray, believe that ye receive them, and ye shall have them"

(Mark 11:24; Matthew 21:22).

"Be careful for nothing; but in everything by prayer and supplication with thanksgiving let your requests be made known unto God"

(Philippians 4:6).

"But let him ask in faith, nothing wavering. For he that wavereth is like a wave of the sea driven with the wind and tossed. For let not that man think that he shall receive anything of the Lord" *(James 1:6, 7).*

"Ye ask, and receive not, because ye ask amiss, that ye may consume it upon your lusts" *(James 4:3).*

Read *How to Pray* and *The Power of Prayer* by R. A. Torrey.

A GOOD CITIZEN OF HEAVEN: OBEYS AND SERVES GOD

If you love Me, OBEY Me *(See: John 14:15, 21, 23).*

Anyone who doesn't OBEY Me, doesn't love Me *(See: John 14:24).*

"... We ought to obey God rather than men" *(Acts 5:29).*

"... Behold, to obey is better than sacrifice ..." *(1 Samuel 15:22).*

When man listens, God speaks; when man OBEYS, God acts.

GUIDELINES FOR OBEDIENCE

"Open thou mine eyes, that I may behold wondrous things out of thy Law" *(Psalm 119:18).*

LAWS of the Kingdom of Heaven:

God's Word (Bible)

The Ten Commandments

(See: Exodus 20:1-17; Deuteronomy 5:6-22).

Jesus said "I am not come to destroy the LAW but to fulfill the LAW" *(Matthew 5:17, 18).* Jesus fulfilled the LAW by obeying it perfectly, fulfilling many of its prophecies and paying the full penalty of the LAW with His death.

The Sermon on the Mount *(See: Matthew 5-7; Luke 6:20-49).*

Jesus' New Commandment: "Love God and your neighbor" *(See: Matthew 22:36-40; Mark 12:28-31; Luke 10:27).*

Do unto others as you would have them do unto you *(See: Matthew 7:12).*

More guidelines: *(See: Ephesians 5:7-32; 5, 6; Colossians 3; 1 Peter 3:1-17; 3, 4).*

JESUS' SHED BLOOD COVERS YOUR INABILITY AND FAILURE TO KEEP THE COMPLETE LAW PERFECTLY.

OBEY THE HOLY SPIRIT

"If we live in the Spirit, let us also walk in the Spirit" *(Galatians 5:25).*

Be LED by the Spirit *(See: Romans 8:14).*

God's LAWS will be written in your heart and mind after Jesus fills you with the Holy Spirit *(See: Hebrews 8:10).*

Be sure that God has first place in your life and make every decision according to what you believe God would want you to do. "Thy will be done."

SAY: "Yes, Lord, I am available and willing." "... Here am I; send me" *(Isaiah 6:8).*

"If any man serve me, let him follow me; and where I am, there shall also my servant be: if any man serve me, him will my Father honour" *(John 12:26).*

All things work together for good to them who fit into God's Plan for their life *(See: Romans 8:28).*

THE TEN COMMANDMENTS

(Exodus 20:3-17)

I Thou shalt have no other gods before Me.

II Thou shalt not make unto thee any graven image, or any likeness of any thing that is in heaven above, or that is in the earth beneath, or that is in the water under the earth: thou shalt not bow down thyself to them, nor serve them: for I the Lord thy God am a jealous God, visiting the iniquity of the fathers upon the children unto the third and fourth generation of them that hate me: and showing mercy unto thousands of them that love Me, and keep My commandments.

III Thou shalt not take the name of the Lord thy God in vain; for the Lord will not hold him guiltless that taketh His name in vain.

IV Remember the Sabbath day, to keep it holy. Six days shalt thou labor, and do all thy work: but the seventh day is the Sabbath of the Lord thy God: in it thou shalt not do any work, thou, nor thy son, nor thy daughter, thy manservant, nor thy maidservant, nor thy cattle, nor thy stranger that is within thy gates: for in six days the Lord made heaven and earth, the sea, and all that in them is, and rested the seventh day: wherefore the Lord blessed the Sabbath day, and hallowed it.

V Honor thy father and thy mother: that thy days may be long upon the land which the Lord thy God giveth thee.

VI Thou shalt not kill.

VII Thou shalt not commit adultery.

VIII Thou shalt not steal.

IX Thou shalt not bear false witness against thy neighbor.

X Thou shalt not covet thy neighbor's house, thou shalt not covet thy neighbor's wife, nor his manservant, nor his maidservant, nor his ox, nor his ass, nor anything that is thy neighbor's.

Each morning ask God to work out His perfect Plan for your life and then yield to Him.

A GOOD CITIZEN OF HEAVEN: CONFESSES SINS

EVERYONE IS A SINNER

"... There is none righteous, no, not one" *(Romans 3:10).*

"For all have sinned, and come short of the glory of God" *(Romans 3:23; 1 John 5:19).*

SIN IS ANYTHING THAT IS CONTRARY TO GOD'S WILL *(See: Matthew 6:10; Romans 14:23; 1 John 5:17; Romans 6, 7, 8).*

There are SINS of COMMISSION: Fornicating, idolatry, adultery, stealing, lying, cheating, and so on *(See: 1 Corinthians 6:9, 10; Galatians 5:19-21; Ephesians 4:14-31; 5:3-12; Colossians 3:5, 8, 9).*

There are SINS of OMISSION: "Therefore to him that knoweth to do good, and doeth it not, to him it is sin" *(James 4:17).*

There are SINS of THE HEART and MIND: Lust, anger, resentment, bitterness, envy, jealousy, hatred and so on. These evil thoughts and desires enter into your mind and heart, and if you cling to them and dwell on them, they will eventually become evil words and deeds.

You must immediately hand all these evil thoughts and feelings over to Jesus, and He will give you His power to conquer them.

"Finally, brethren, whatsoever things are true, whatsoever things are honest, whatsoever things are just, whatsoever things are pure, whatsoever things are lovely, whatsoever things are of good report; if there be any virtue, and if there be any praise, think on these things"

(Philippians 4:8).

Legally, Jesus has washed all your SINS away, past, present, and future, but in actual practice, you still SIN *(See: 1 Peter 2:24; Isaiah 1:18).*

But, you don't *have* to sin *(See: 1 John 2:1; Jude 1:24).*

Satan tempts and encourages you to SIN, and when you do, he has the authority and power to send his demons to attack you. God, however, uses the evil Satan brings against you for good *(See: Acts 5:1-11; 1 Timothy 1:20; John 5:14; Romans 8:28; 1 Corinthians 5:5; Matthew 9:2-5).*

Believers can be afflicted by Satan only as God permits *(See: Job 1:12; 2:4-7).*

UNCONFESSED SIN BREAKS YOUR FELLOWSHIP WITH GOD *(See: Isaiah 59:2).*

"... But if we confess our sins, he is faithful and just to forgive us our sins, and to cleanse us from all unrighteousness" *(1 John 1:9).*

When you confess your SINS, Satan must call his demons to retreat from tormenting you, and you can then ask God to heal you and your circumstances *(See: James 5:14-16).*

In some cases the natural consequences of your SIN must run its normal course. For example:

Even after you confess your SINS, Satan sometimes can still attack you through other people, reminding you of your sinful past.

A GOOD CITIZEN OF HEAVEN: LOVES GOD AND HIS NEIGHBORS AND HIS ENEMIES

Tell God that you LOVE HIM:

"Jesus said unto him, Thou shalt love the Lord thy God with all thy heart, and with all thy soul, and with all thy mind. This is the first and great commandment. And the second is like unto it, thou shalt love thy neighbor as thyself. On these two commandments hang all the law and the prophets" *(Matthew 22:37-40; 2 John 5).*

"But I say unto you which hear, Love your enemies, do good to them which hate you, Bless them that curse you, and pray for them which despitefully use you" *(Luke 6:27, 28).*

"... The love of God is shed abroad in our hearts by the Holy Ghost which is given unto us" *(Romans 5:5).*

"And we know that all things work together for good to them that love God, to them who are the called according to his purpose" *(Romans 8:28).*

A GOOD CITIZEN OF HEAVEN: TRUSTS GOD

"Trust in the Lord with all thine heart; and

lean not unto thine own understanding. In all thy ways acknowledge him, and he shall direct thy paths" *(Proverbs 3:5, 6).*

"Though he slay me, yet will I trust in him ..." *(Job 13:15).*

When you WORRY and COMPLAIN about your troubles, you are NOT TRUSTING God, but you are giving Satan an opportunity to increase them.

When you PRAY about your troubles, you ARE TRUSTING God and are turning your troubles over to Him, and He can handle them.

A GOOD CITIZEN OF HEAVEN: FORGIVES AND DOES NOT JUDGE

"Judge not, and ye shall not be judged: condemn not, and ye shall not be condemned: forgive, and ye shall be forgiven"

(Luke 6:37; Matthew 6:14; 1 Corinthians 11:31).

"And when ye stand praying, forgive, if ye have ought against any: that your Father also which is in heaven may forgive you your trespasses. But if ye do not forgive, neither will your Father which is in heaven forgive your trespasses" *(Mark 11:25, 26).*

"And be ye kind one to another, tender-hearted, forgiving one another, even as God for Christ's sake hath forgiven you"

(Ephesians 4:32).

JUDGE YOURSELF: "For if we would judge ourselves, we should not be judged" *(1 Corinthians 11:31; Matthew 7:3-5; Luke 6:41, 42).*

A GOOD CITIZEN OF HEAVEN: GIVES

"Give, and it shall be given unto you; good measure, pressed down, and shaken together, and running over, shall men give into your bosom. For with the same measure that ye mete withal it shall be measured to you again"

(Luke 6:38).

"But this I say, He which soweth sparingly shall reap also sparingly; and he which soweth bountifully shall reap also bountifully. Every man according as he purposeth in his heart, so let him give; not grudgingly, or of necessity: for God loveth a cheerful giver"

(2 Corinthians 9:6, 7).

"I have shewed you all things, how that so labouring ye ought to support the weak, and to remember the words of the Lord Jesus, how he said, It is more blessed to give than to receive" *(Acts 20:35).*

A GOOD CITIZEN OF HEAVEN: GROWS SPIRITUALLY

With the Holy Spirit living inside, Christians can be growing in the fruit of the Spirit: love, joy, peace, patience, kindness, faithfulness, goodness, humility, and discipline.

The Holy Spirit develops this fruit in the Christians in whom He dwells, gradually bringing them into the image of Christ.

> For the perfecting of the saints, for the work of the ministry, for the edifying of the body of Christ: Till we all come in the unity of the faith, and of the knowledge of the Son of God, unto a perfect man, unto the measure of the stature of the fulness of Christ: That we henceforth be no more children, tossed to and fro, and carried about with every wind of doctrine,

by the sleight of men, and cunning craftiness, whereby they lie in wait to deceive; But speaking the truth in love, may grow up into him in all things, which is the head, even Christ"

(Ephesians 4:12-15).

Having the Holy Spirit dwelling inside you is absolutely essential to your Christian growth. The Holy Spirit teaches, guides, and leads you.

A GOOD CITIZEN OF HEAVEN: FELLOWSHIPS WITH OTHER BELIEVERS

Go to a good Bible-believing church

(See: Acts 2:42).

"Not forsaking the assembling of ourselves together ..." *(Hebrews 10:25).*

"For where two or three are gathered together in my name, there am I in the midst of them" *(Matthew 18:20).*

Join a Bible-study-group of people who believe God's Word is true *(See: John 17:17; Psalms 119:160).*

Christian brothers and sisters should help each other as they study their Citizenship Manuals (Bible).

Christian brothers and sisters correct each other when needed *(See: 1 Thessalonians 5:11-15).*

Christian brothers and sisters help each other stay on the straight and narrow path *(See: Hebrews 10:25; Colossians 3:16).*

It is much easier for an isolated Christian to drift off into error. Satan knows this and takes advantage of it.

A GOOD CITIZEN OF HEAVEN: LEARNS AND SINGS HIS COUNTRY'S PATRIOTIC SONGS

"Speaking to yourselves in psalms and hymns and spiritual songs, singing and making melody in your heart to the Lord" *(Ephesians 5:19).*

"Let the word of Christ dwell in you richly in all wisdom; teaching and admonishing one another in psalms and hymns and spiritual songs, singing with grace in your hearts to the Lord" *(Colossians 3:16)*.

"And when they [Jesus and his disciples] had sung an hymn, they went out into the mount of Olives" *(Matthew 26:30)*.

PRAISE SONGS

For example: "Gloria Patri"

Glory be to the Father, and to the Son, and to the Holy Ghost; As it was in the beginning, is now and ever shall be, world without end. Amen, Amen.

"Doxology"

Praise God from whom all blessings flow, praise him all creatures here below, praise him above you heavenly host, praise Father, Son, and Holy Ghost. Amen.

A GOOD CITIZEN OF HEAVEN: FASTS

FASTING is putting the flesh under the authority of the Spirit, by willfully not eating a meal or meals in order to focus your attention upon the Lord.

FASTING can be used to reinforce special prayer requests.

FASTING HINTS: Give up something you enjoy but is bad for you. Do it as unto the Lord *(See: Colossians 3:17, 23).*

JESUS' ADVICE ON FASTING:

"Moreover when ye fast, be not as the hypocrites, of a sad countenance: for they disfigure their faces, that they may appear unto men to fast. Verily I say unto you, They have their reward. But thou, when thou fastest, anoint thine head, and wash thy face; That thou appear not unto men to fast, but unto thy Father, which is in secret: and thy Father, which seeth in secret, shall reward thee openly *(Matthew 6:16-18).*

A GOOD CITIZEN OF HEAVEN: REJOICES

"Rejoice and leap for joy when men hate you and reproach you, for your reward in heaven is great" *(Luke 6:22, 23).*

"But rejoice, inasmuch as ye are partakers of Christ's sufferings; that, when his glory shall be revealed, ye may be glad also with exceeding joy" *(1 Peter 4:13).*

"Rejoice, in the Lord always: and again I say, rejoice" *(Philippians 4:4).*

"... Rejoice, because your names are written in heaven" (*Luke 10:20*).

"Whom [Jesus] having not seen, ye love; in whom, though now ye see him not, yet believing, ye rejoice with joy unspeakable and full of glory" (*1 Peter 1:8*).

Read *The Christian's Secret of a Happy Life,* by Hannah Whitall Smith.

A GOOD CITIZEN OF HEAVEN: BLESSES ISRAEL

God gave us the Bible through the Jewish people.

God gave us Jesus through the Jews.

GOD SAID TO ABRAM: "And I will bless them that bless thee, and curse him that curseth thee: and in thee shall all families of the earth be blessed (*Genesis 12:3; Acts 3:25*).

GOD SAID TO JACOB: "... Cursed be every one that curseth thee, and blessed be he that blesseth thee" (*Genesis 27:29*).

GOD SAID TO ISRAEL: "Blessed is he that blesseth thee, and cursed is he that curseth thee" (*Numbers 24:9*).

GOD SAID TO JERUSALEM: "For thus saith the Lord of hosts; After the glory hath he sent me unto the nations which spoiled you: for he that toucheth you toucheth the apple of his eye. For, behold, I will shake mine hand upon them, and they shall be a spoil to their servants: and ye shall know that the Lord of hosts hath sent me" *(Zechariah 2:8, 9).*

A GOOD CITIZEN OF HEAVEN: LAYS UP TREASURES IN HEAVEN

"Set your affection on things above, not on things on earth" *(Colossians 3:2; Romans 8:5).*

"Lay not up for yourselves treasures upon earth, where moth and rust doth corrupt, and where thieves break through and steal: But lay up for yourselves treasures in heaven, where neither moth nor rust doth corrupt, and where thieves do not break through nor steal: For where your treasure is there will your heart be also" *(Matthew 6:19-21; Luke 12:33; 1 Peter 1:4).*

"Blessed are ye, when men shall revile you, and persecute you, and shall say all manner of evil against you falsely, for my sake. Rejoice, and be exceeding glad: for great is your reward in heaven: for so persecuted they the prophets which were before you" *(Matthew 5:11, 12; Luke 6:22, 23).*

"And whatsoever ye do, do it heartily, as to the Lord, and not unto men; Knowing that of the Lord ye shall receive the reward of the inheritance: for ye serve the Lord Christ"

(Colossians 3:23, 24).

BEHAVIOR TO WIN REWARDS:

(See: Colossians 3; Ephesians 4:7-32; 5, 6; 1 Peter 3:1-17; 2 Peter 1:4-8).

Do all the things listed under "A Good Citizen of Heaven," pages 61-88.

"For the Son of man shall come in the glory of his Father with his angels; and then he shall reward every man according to his works" *(Matthew 16:27).*

A GOOD CITIZEN OF HEAVEN: WITNESSES TO OTHERS

TELL others who your king and Lord is (the triune God) and what country you belong to (heaven) *(See: Acts 1:8).*

"Whosoever therefore shall confess me before men, him will I confess also before my Father which is in heaven. But whosoever shall deny me before men, him will I also deny before my Father which is in heaven"

(Matthew 10:32, 33; Luke 12:8, 9).

A GOOD CITIZEN OF HEAVEN: RECRUITS NEW CITIZENS FOR HEAVEN

HELP others to escape from Satan's evil clutches and into Jesus' welcoming arms

(See: Proverbs 11:30).

TELL others about Jesus and His Kingdom and INVITE them into the Kingdom to partake of God's fruit, gifts, and eternal life

(See: 1 Peter 3:15).

A GOOD CITIZEN OF HEAVEN:

Is water baptized.
Communicates with God: listens to God, talks to God.
Trusts God.
Forgives and does not judge.
Grows spiritually.
Learns and sings his country's patriotic songs.
Blesses Israel.
Witnesses to others.
Recruits new citizens for heaven.
Takes communion.
Obeys and serves God.
Confesses sins.
Loves God and his neighbor and his enemies.
Gives.
Fellowships with other believers.
Fasts.
Rejoices
Lays up treasures in heaven.

Immigration Into Heaven

IMMIGRATION INTO HEAVEN

God will bring you into the physical Kingdom of heaven at the proper time, which He will decide. Since you do not know the time of your immigration into heaven, try to be ready at all times to make this trip to your home country.

Don't bother packing a bag, because you can't take any material possessions with you. You should pack up spiritual things in your mind, soul, and spirit to carry with you into heaven.

One thing you can take with you is FRUIT (Fruit of the Spirit): love, joy, peace, patience, kindness, faithfulness, goodness, humility, and discipline. All other necessary things will be provided for you.

NO MORE DUAL CITIZENSHIP

When you emigrate from the earthly kingdom and immigrate into the heavenly Kingdom, this ends your dual citizenship. Your citizenship on earth ends at this time, and you are now totally and completely a citizen of heaven, where you will spend eternity.

YOU WILL ENTER THE KINGDOM OF HEAVEN IN ONE OF TWO WAYS:

1. Physical death (death of your body) *(See: Hebrews 9:27).*
2. Rapture or translation (ascending bodily into heaven) *(See: 1 Thessalonians 4:16-18; Matthew 24:36-51).*

1. PHYSICAL DEATH. When you die physically, you will temporarily leave your body behind, but it will later be restored into a beautiful immortal body and returned to you radiant, new, and perfect. It will be similar to Jesus' body after He was resurrected from the dead *(See: Philippians 3:20, 21)*

YOU — your personality, mind and emotions-will — and newborn spirit will go into Heaven and live forever. You will be given a spirit body *(See: 1 Corinthians 15:35-50).*

You will be escorted to your place in heaven by angels and probably by loved ones who have preceded you into heaven. You will be welcomed by God the Father, God the Son, and God the Holy spirit. You will be welcomed with much joy and gladness. You will be given a white robe and crowns.

"Precious in the sight of the Lord is the death of his saints" *(Psalm 116:15).*

2. RAPTURE or TRANSLATION. There is another way that you can enter heaven in this period near the end of time. You bypass death and ascend bodily and meet Jesus in the air and are escorted into heaven by Jesus and the angels. This event, which occurs before The Great Tribulation (described in Revelation) is known as the Rapture, when Christian believers on earth will be taken up into heaven.

Your mortal body will be instantly transformed into your new, glorified, immortal body *(See: 1 Corinthians 15:51-53).*

Some believers have disappeared and no bodies were ever found, because God took them to heaven: Enoch *(Genesis 5:24)* and Elijah *(2 Kings 2:11),* and Jesus' ascension *(Mark 16:19; Luke 24:50, 51).*

You will be welcomed into heaven by God the Father, God the Son, and God the Holy Spirit, and the angels and all inhabitants of heaven. You are coming home, where you are loved and wanted by God and all your fellow citizens.

Unbelievers left on earth will experience

seven years of tribulation while God's judgment is directed upon the earth and its inhabitants because of SIN *(See: Luke 21:10, 11, 25, 26; Revelation 6-19).*

GENERAL INFORMATION

IMMUNIZATIONS — You have already been innoculated against the disease of SIN. NO other immunizations are necessary to enter heaven, because there are NO diseases in heaven. Also your new body will not be subject to sickness, disease, or injury.

HEALTH INSURANCE — Since there is no sickness or disease of any kind in heaven, there is no need for health insurance.

CUSTOMS SERVICE — There are NO customs requirements in heaven, because you will be taking nothing with you. All earthly possessions are left behind, even your old body. You won't need them. All will be provided for you, even a new body

(See: 2 Peter 1:8, 11).

Even the gifts of the Spirit will no longer be needed. But the fruit of the Spirit will go with you as part of your treasure in heaven. There will be rewards and crowns waiting for you.

Your soul (mind, emotions, and will) and live spirit go with you.

TREASURY — NO treasury regulations. No money will be needed. In heaven you will have everything you need and want, FREE.

AGRICULTURE — NO agriculture regulations are required, because you will not be taking any agricultural products with you into heaven. You will not need to eat in heaven, but you may eat delicious food provided for you, if you wish. Plenty of food will be available. Eating is not necessary but is optional.

ESCORT INTO HEAVEN

JESUS CHRIST,
The Lord of Heaven and Earth

Hereby assures that heavenly angels and heavenly saints (friends and relatives) already residing in heaven, will assist, escort, and protect this heavenly national named herein to pass without delay or hindrance and will give all lawful aid and protection, through hostile territory (Satan's domain — earth and its atmosphere) and into the heavenly kingdom at the time that this citizen's earthly body dies or ascends into heaven at the Rapture.

TENURE (length of stay)	ETERNITY (forever)

NO ALIENS (those who reject Christ) will be admitted into heaven.

Facts About God, Your New Ruler, King, and Lord

WHO IS GOD?

"Know therefore this day, and consider it in thine heart, that the Lord he is God in heaven above, and upon the earth beneath: there is none else" *(Deuteronomy 4:39).*

GOD IS:

God is the great "I AM" *(See: Exodus 3:14).*

God is self-existent *(See: Revelation 22:13; Deuteronomy 4:35, 39).*

God is the CREATOR of all things *(See: Genesis 1, 2; Revelation 4:11; Isaiah 66:2).*

God is the CREATOR and RULER of the UNIVERSE *(See: Acts 17:24-26; Psalms 103:19).*

God is the only ONE in the Universe WHO was not Created.

God is high above all creatures and things *(See: Isaiah 44:6, 8; 2 Chronicles 2:5).*

God is the SOURCE of all good *(See: Luke 18:19; James 1:17).*

God is SPIRIT (not limited by a body) *(See: John 4:24).*

God is LIGHT *(See: 1 John 1:5).*

God is a PERSON. He feels, thinks, loves, desires.

God is a TRIUNE GOD *(See: 1 John 5:7; Matthew 28:19; 2 Corinthians 13:14; 1 Peter 1:2; Jude 20, 21).*

God the Father,
God the Son (Jesus),
God the Holy Spirit.

Three Persons united with ONE PURPOSE, ONE AIM, ONE GOAL — ONE PERFECT CHARACTER — ONE GOD.

WHERE IS GOD?

God's THRONE is in HEAVEN. He rules the universe from heaven. Heaven is God's throne, and earth is His footstool

(See: Acts 7:49; Luke 11:2; Isaiah 66:1; Matthew 5:34, 35; Joshua 2:11; Ecclesiastes 5:2; Deuteronomy 4:39; Psalm 103:19).

God is EVERYWHERE:

"Am I a God at hand, saith the Lord, and not a God afar off? Can any hide himself in secret places that I shall not see him? saith the Lord. Do not I fill heaven and earth? saith the Lord" *(Jeremiah 23:23, 24).*

"Whither shall I go from thy spirit? or whither shall I flee from thy presence? If I ascend up into heaven, thou art there; if I make my bed in hell, behold, thou art there. If I take the wings of the morning, and dwell in the uttermost parts of the sea; Even there shall thy hand lead me, and thy right hand shall hold me" *(Psalm 139:7-10).*

"Who coverest thyself with light as with a garment: who stretchest out the heavens like a curtain: Who layeth the beams of his chambers in the waters: who maketh the clouds his chariot: who walketh upon the wings of the wind" *(Psalm 104:2, 3).*

WHAT IS GOD LIKE?

DESCRIPTION OF GOD:

God is ETERNAL AND IMMORTAL — Unlimited by time; has always existed; will always exist; no beginning and no end *(See: Psalm 90:1; 145:13; Revelation 1:8, 11; 4:8-10; 1 Timothy 1:17; 6:16).*

God possesses ALL KNOWLEDGE — He knows everything that is happening, has happened, and will happen *(See: Romans 11:33).*

God is ALL-WISE — He understands everything *(See: Proverbs 3:19; Daniel 2:20-22; Colossians 2:2, 3).*

God is PERSONALLY PRESENT EVERY-WHERE — Unlimited by space *(See: Jeremiah 23:23, 24; 1 John 4:15; Matthew 18:20).*

God is INVISIBLE *(See: John 1:18; 5:37; Colossians 1:15; 1 Timothy 1:17).*

God is ALL-POWERFUL — Nothing is impossible with God *(See: Genesis 18:14; Mark 10:27; Luke 1:37; 18:27; Matthew 19:26).*

God DOES NOT FAINT and is NOT WEARY *(See: Isaiah 40:28).*

God NEVER CHANGES *(See: Hebrews 1:12; 13:8; Psalm 102:26, 27; James 1:17).*

God is ABSOLUTE TRUTH *(See: 1 John 5:6; John 14:6; 17:3; Jeremiah 10:10).*

God is GLORIOUS and MAJESTIC *(See: 1 Chronicles 29:11; Matthew 6:13; Psalm 45:3; Jude 25).*

On earth, God purposely limits His presence for our sakes; we MORTAL beings could not survive looking at God's full glorious presence *(See: Exodus 33:20-23).*

GOD'S PERSONALITY:

God is strong and firm but also gentle and kind.

God is a Person with feelings and emotions. God can be HAPPY, REGRETFUL, or SORROWFUL.

God is LOVE — He gives everyone unlimited, unconditional love, even His enemies *(See: John 3:16; Romans 5:8; 8:39).*

God is MERCIFUL *(See: Exodus 34:6; Deuteronomy 4:31; 5:10).*

God is FORGIVING *(See: Ephesians 4:32; Luke 15:11-32).*

God is COMPASSIONATE *(See: 2 Kings 13:23; Psalm 103:13, 14).*

God is LONG-SUFFERING — Patient *(See: Numbers 14:18; 2 Peter 3:9).*

God is GRACIOUS — Gives unmerited favor *(See: Exodus 34:6; Psalm 116:5).*

God is UNSELFISH, UNDERSTANDING, KIND, TENDER, and CARING.

God has IMAGINATION and HUMOR.

God is a JEALOUS GOD *(See: Exodus 20:5; 34:14; Deuteronomy 4:24; 5:9; 6:15).*

God can become ANGRY *(See: Deuteronomy 1:34, 35; 3:26; 4:21; Jeremiah 44:6, 8).*

God is a CONSUMING FIRE *(See: Hebrews 12:29; Deuteronomy 4:24; 5:4, 5; 9:3).*

Jesus is God INCARNATE (God in a physical body).

God's HEART'S DESIRE is to give you a happy home in His eternal Kingdom.

For further information concerning God's attributes, read: *What is God Like?* by Eugenia Price; Chapter 1, "Our Father," in *A Layman Looks at the Lord's Prayer*, by W. Phillip Keller.

GOD'S CHARACTER:

God is MORALLY PERFECT — His motives are always pure *(See: Matthew 5:48).*

GOOD, and all good comes from God *(See: Luke 18:19; James 1:17).*

UPRIGHT *(See: Psalm 25:8; 92:15).*

RIGHTEOUS *(See: Isaiah 5:16; Ezra 9:15; Psalm 145:17).*

HOLY *(See: Psalm 99:9).*

UNCORRUPTIBLE — God never does anything that is dishonest or deceitful *(See: Deuteronomy 32:4)*

God is ABSOLUTE TRUTH *(See: 1 John 5:6; John 14:6; 17:3; Jeremiah 10:10).*

God is ABSOLUTELY TRUSTWORTHY — He can be trusted *(See: Proverbs 3:5, 6).*

God is FAITHFUL — He is loyal *(See: 1 Corinthians 10:13; 1 Peter 4:19; Deuteronomy 7:9).*

God is JUST — He is never unfair and always judges fairly *(See: Isaiah 9:7; 45:20-25; 1 John 1:9; Deuteronomy 32:4).*

The world's human value system is based on the day-to-day struggle to survive and prosper; sin warps and limits our perspective.

But God has His own perfect value system, based on His eternal perspective. God's law is above and beyond our laws; His law is based upon His own moral integrity.

Facts About Your Future Heavenly Home

WHY IS THERE A HEAVEN?

Heaven is for God's throne *(See: Isaiah 66:1; Acts 7:49).*

Also God made heaven as a home country for all those who choose Him. It is a place where all His children will be welcome and happy, after they leave the Earth at death or at the Rapture. Heaven is where you belong.

WHO RULES OVER HEAVEN?

God rules over heaven with love and justice.

WHAT IS HEAVEN'S ENVIRONMENT LIKE?

Heaven has the perfect environment:

Beautiful — without diseases, or death.

Cleanliness — nothing unclean.

Clean, pure, air — NO pollution — clean, pure water.

Perfect environment — NO stench, NO disagreeable odors.

Perfect temperature — never too cold, never too hot *(See: Revelation 7:16).*

Perfect humidity.

Beautiful music of praise and worship to the Lord.

Always light — NO darkness, NO night.

NO environmental uncertainties, disasters, problems or calamities: NO storms, NO tornadoes, NO volcanos, NO droughts, NO floods, NO hurricanes, NO earthquakes, NO fires.

The tree of life is in the midst of paradise *(See: Revelation 2:7; 22:2, 14).*

Heaven has a pure river of water of life, clear as crystal *(See: Revelation 22:1).*

A re-created earth, restored to its original beauty, will be a part of our heavenly residence *(See: 2 Peter 3:13; Revelation 21:1).*

WHAT IS HEAVEN LIKE?

TIME — All of time through eternity is yours to enjoy. Just relax — NO rushing, NO hurrying, NO deadlines. An EVERLASTING Kingdom *(See: Psalm 145:13).*

DWELLINGS IN HEAVEN:

God has made beautiful houses for His family members to enjoy *(See: John 14:2; 2 Corinthians 5:1).*

A beautiful New Jerusalem will be the city of heaven:

> And I John saw the holy city, new Jerusalem, coming down from God out of heaven, prepared as a bride adorned for her husband. ...
>
> And he carried me away in the spirit to a great and high mountain, and shewed me that great city, the holy Jerusalem, descending out of heaven from God. Having the glory of God: and her light was like unto a stone most precious, even like a jasper stone, clear as crystal; And had a wall great and high, and had twelve gates, and at the gates twelve angels, and names written thereon, which are the names of the twelve tribes of the children of Israel: On the east three gates; on the north three gates; on the south three gates; and on the west three gates. And the wall of the city had twelve foundations, and in them the names of the twelve apostles of the Lamb.

And he that talked with me had a golden reed to measure the city, and the gates thereof, and the wall thereof. And the city lieth foursquare, and the length is as large as the breadth: and he measured the city with the reed, twelve thousand furlongs [1,500 miles square]. The length and the breadth and the height of it are equal. And he measured the wall thereof, an hundred and forty and four cubits [216 feet], according to the measure of a man, that is, of the angel. And the building of the wall of it was of jasper: and the city was pure gold, like unto clear glass. And the foundations of the wall of the city were garnished with all manner of precious stones, the first foundation was jasper; the second, sapphire; the third a chaledony; the fourth, an emerald; The fifth, sardonyx; the sixth, sardius; the seventh, chrysolyte; the eighth, beryl; the ninth, a topaz; the tenth, a chrysoprasus; the eleventh, a jacinth; the twelfth, an amethyst. And the twelve gates were twelve pearls; every several gate was of one pearl: and the street of the city was pure gold, as it were transparent glass. And I saw no temple therein: for the Lord God Almighty and the Lamb are the temple of it. And the city had no need of the sun, neither of the moon, to shine in it: for the glory of God did lighten it, and the Lamb is the light thereof. And the nations of them which are saved shall walk in the light of it: and the kings of the earth do bring their glory and honour into it. And the gates of it shall not be shut at all by day: for there shall be no night there. And they shall bring the glory and honour of the nations into it. And there shall in no wise enter into it any thing that defileth, neither whatsoever worketh abomination, or maketh a lie: but they which are written in the Lamb's book of life *(Revelation 21:2, 10-27).*

WHO WILL BE IN HEAVEN?

GOD, ANGELS, ALL BELIEVERS, ANIMALS:

GOD — "Thus saith the Lord, the heaven is my throne ..." *(Isaiah 66:1; Matthew 5:16; 1 Kings 8:30).*

ANGELS — The angels call heaven home; it's where they return after their assignments on earth are completed *(See: Matthew 28:2; Luke 22:43; John 1:51; Revelation 10:1; 18:1; 20:1).*

ALL BELIEVERS — All those written in the Lamb's book of life *(See: Revelation 21:27).* "Great multitudes of all nations, kindreds and people" *(Revelation 7:9).*

ANIMALS — All animals will be gentle and will not eat flesh, nor will they be eaten by people. They will have NO diseases or sickness, and they will NOT die *(See: Isaiah 11:6-8).*

WHO WILL NOT BE IN HEAVEN?

Nothing that defiles, works abomination, or makes a lie — all those who are NOT written in the Lamb's book of life *(See: Revelation 21:27).*

No UNBELIEVERS will BE IN heaven.

Satan and his demons WILL NOT BE in heaven.

WHAT WILL YOU AND YOUR FELLOW CITIZENS BE LIKE IN HEAVEN?

BODY:

You will have a spirit body that will be shining, and possibly vaporous.

This body will always be perfect:

PERFECT HEALTH

Never sick or injured, no medicine will ever be needed. The services of doctors, nurses, and hospitals will not be necessary. Never die — NO death

(See: 1 Corinthians 15:42).

PERFECT COMFORT

Never suffer pain. Never tired or weary. Never hungry or thirsty

(See: Revelation 7:16, 17).

Your body will not need food or drink, but they will be available for your pleasure: water, wine, bread, fruit, and so on.

PERFECT FIVE SENSES

The five senses will be enhanced, and possibly other senses will be added.

STRONG AND POWERFUL

NO weakness — NO tiredness

(See: 1 Corinthians 15:43; Revelation 7:15).

In your immortal glorified body you may now look at God face-to-face

(See: 1 Corinthians 13:12).

BEAUTIFUL

Your new body will be very beautiful, shining and bright *(See: Daniel 12:3).*

Your NEW BODY will resemble your original mortal body — you will be recognizable.

Your NEW BODY will rejoin your soul and spirit and house them.

Your NEW BODY will not be subject to lustful desires *(See: 1 Corinthians 15:43).*

Your NEW BODY will be like Christ's resurrected body *(See: 1 John 3:2; Philippians 3:20, 21; Luke 24:26-43; 1 Corinthians 15:44, 48, 49).*

Jesus' name will be in your forehead *(See: Revelation 22:4).*

Residents of heaven will be in various stages of development. There will be: babes, children, adolescents, and adults.

CLOTHING:

You will be clothed in lovely, white linen garments, and you will have a beautiful crown to wear *(See: Revelation 2:10; 7:9; 19:8, 14).*

MIND AND EMOTIONS:

MIND

Your mind will be free from earthly restrictions or limitations. Clear thinking — pure thoughts. Decisions will be made based on solid facts and truth. NO confusion, NO forgetfulness. NO addictions, NO bad dreams. NO boredom, NO monotony. NO phobias, NO mental illness.

EMOTIONS

Complete serenity, tranquility, contentment, and peace of mind. Joy, happiness, and love.

NO crying, unhappiness, sadness, sorrow, mourning, or grief

(See: Revelation 7:17).

NO loneliness, NO good-byes, NO separations. NO discouragement, doubts, discontent, depression, or despair. NO worries about health, money, food, or relationships. NO anxieties, nervousness, pressures, tensions, hassles, or troubles. NO hatred, anger, bad temper, arguing, conflicts, discord, misunderstandings, resentments, bitterness, or hurt feelings. NO temptations, envy, or jealousy. NO fear. NO frustrations. NO disappointments, disillusionments, regrets, or guilt.

MORALITY:

Spiritual growth — we will love God more completely, because we will see Him face-to-face

(See: 1 John 3:2, 3).

High morality will prevail *(See: 2 Peter 3:13):*

Openness, trustworthiness, truthfulness, and honesty. Fairness and justice. Love, kindness, goodness, compassion, gentleness, and forgiveness. Patience. Humility. Self-control. Faithfulness, loyalty, and dependability. Courage. Industriousness. Order.

NO EVIL — Satan and his demons are banished from heaven. In the absence of Satan and his demons, there will be NO SIN: NO crime, stealing, swindling, graft, dishonesty. NO coveting, jealousy, greed, lust, pride, or temptations. NO lying, cheating, scheming, or craftiness. NO treachery, deceit, double-crossing, or betrayal. NO gossip or backbiting. NO temper, threats, hatred, killing, cruelty, or anger. NO fighting, wars, killing, tyranny, or chaos. NO distrust, injustice, unfairness, or misjudgments. NO dissension, disharmony, complaining, rudeness, unreasonableness, divisiveness, or animosity. NO laziness or carelessness. NO error, NO mistakes. NO cowardice. NO selfishness, unkindness, wrong or bad attitudes, or misrepresenting.

PERFECT GOVERNMENT

Jesus is KING — "... The government shall be upon his shoulder, ... Wonderful, Counsellor ... Prince of Peace." Of this government there will be NO END

(Isaiah 9:6, 7; Luke 1:32, 33).

WHAT WILL YOU DO IN HEAVEN?

ACTIVITIES IN HEAVEN:

A QUICK REVIEW OF YOUR LIFE

Like a movie. NO judgments. NO recriminations. This will be for your edification.

PLEASANT DUTIES AND RESPONSIBILITIES

Teaching. Positions of service. You will be given duties commensurate with your qualifications *(See: Matthew 25:21, 23).*

Perhaps renovating the universe and ruling over other worlds. Perhaps ruling over cities and kingdoms of the earth's millennial kingdom. There will be NO drudgery work.

COMMUNICATION

You will speak a heavenly language ... universal praise of Jesus, the Lamb of God, and of God the Father *(See: Revelation 5:12-14; 7:9, 10).*

You may also communicate by thought transfer or thought projection.

TRAVEL

Walk short distances. For longer trips, you may be able to float, fly, and travel through the universe instantly. Go through solid substances, and appear and disappear at will *(See: John 20:19, 26; Acts 8:39, 40; Luke 24:31, 36).*

NO vehicles will be needed.

EATING FOR PLEASURE

Eat bread in the Kingdom *(See: Luke 14:15).*
Drink wine *(See: Mark 14:25; Luke 22:18).*
Eat fruit of the tree of life *(See: Revelation 2:7; 22:14).*

Drink the water of life *(See: Revelation 21:6; 22:17).*

Apparently, NO meat will be eaten.

SINGING, MUSIC, AND PRAISING

Children will play and sing. Adults will make music: Others will play harps *(See: Revelation 14:2).* Many will sing praises to the Lord *(See: Revelation 5:9; 14:3).*

Read *Seeing the Invisible,* by Anne Sandberg.

REWARDS IN HEAVEN

"I am thy exceeding great reward" *(Genesis 15:1).*

"Him that overcometh I will make a pillar in the temple of my God ..." *(Revelation 3:12).*

"To him that overcometh will I grant to sit

with me in my throne, even as I also overcame, and am set down with my Father in His throne" *(Revelation 3:21).*

Rewards for the righteous *(See: Psalm 58:11).*

Rewards according to your works *(See: Matthew 16:27).*

Rewards according to your own labor *(See: 1 Corinthians 3:8).*

Rewards to those who diligently seek God *(See: Hebrews 11:6).*

Rewards for secretly fasting and praying *(See: Matthew 6:6, 18).*

Rewards for secretly giving alms *(See: Matthew 6:4).*

Rewards of a prophet for receiving a prophet *(See: Matthew 10:41).*

Reward of a righteous man for receiving a righteous man *(See: Matthew 10:41).*

Reward for giving a cup of cold water to a little child *(See: Matthew 10:42).*

Rewards for helping God's children *(See: Hebrews 6:10).*

Rewards for those who give up home, brothers, sisters, father, mother, or wife to follow Jesus *(See: Matthew 19:29).*

CROWNS

Crown of life — a martyr's crown *(See: Revelation 2:10).*

To those who resist temptation *(See: James 1:12).*

Crown of righteousness — to those who look forward to Christ's return *(See: 2 Timothy 4:8).*

Crown of glory — to faithful ministers *(See: 1 Peter 5:4; 1 Corinthians 3:10-15).*

Incorruptible crown — to those who strive to do God's will *(See: 1 Corinthians 9:25).*

Soul-winner's crown — to those who win souls to Christ *(See: Philippians 4:1; 1 Thessalonians 2:19).*

SUMMARY OF HEAVEN

God will open wide the gates of heaven for you to enter into the eternal Kingdom of our Lord *(See: 2 Peter 1:11).*

Heaven is the eternal home of all God's children. Heaven is your home country; it's where you belong.

God will be your Father; Jesus will be your elder brother.

God the Holy Spirit will be your guide and teacher.

The angels will be your companions and helpers.

You will be surrounded by your fellow-believer brothers and sisters, who love you.

God has made heaven a perfect environment for you. It is fantastically beautiful, with an atmosphere of love, joy, peace, happiness, and freedom *(See: 1 Corinthians 2:9; Isaiah 64:4).*

The new earth will be a part of future heaven: "Nevertheless we, according to his promise, look for new heavens and a new earth, wherein dwelleth righteousness" *(2 Peter 3:13; Revelation 21:1).*

God's heart's desire is to make you happy. God and His angels will spend eternity watching over you and seeing that your every need and desire are provided for. You will have access to all the riches of His Domain.

Be very certain that you have met all of your "passport" requirements as explained in the two sections "How to Become a Citizen of Heaven," pages 22-28, and "Becoming a Citizen of Heaven," pages 30-38, so that you will be ready at all times (date unknown) for your trip to heaven. You will be glad you did.

HAPPY ETERNITY!